My Good Friend

by Nina Valenti
Illustrated by Don Dyen

Glenview, Illinois • Boston, Massachusetts • Chandler, Arizona
Upper Saddle River, New Jersey

My name is Sasha. I have a story to tell. One morning my teacher, Mrs. Ferrara, told my class that a new student was joining our class. "Her name is Luz," said Mrs. Ferrara. "She likes math and music. Luz doesn't see the same way you do."

folding cane

Luz walked into our classroom. She had a long cane in her hand. I think she uses it to help her feel things she can't see. Mrs. Ferrara gave her a seat in the front of the room, close to the board. Her desk was far from the window. I think the glaring light from the window bothered her.

---

cane: a walking stick

computer

   Then another teacher, Mr. Timms, came
in. He gave Luz a small computer. It had a
special light. I saw that the words on the
computer screen were larger than usual.
Later Mr. Timms gave Luz something to
make the words in her books look bigger.

José tried to help Luz walk downstairs. Luz said, "Thanks, but I don't need help."

I introduced myself at lunch. "Hi, Luz, I am Sasha. I came from Russia last year." She answered quietly, "Hi, Sasha. I was born in California. My parents are from Mexico."

I thought Luz looked sad. One day, I asked her, "Why are you sad, Luz?"

She looked at me for a minute. Then she said, "I miss my old school. My friends knew what I could and could not do. They knew when I needed help and when I did not."

miss: feel unhappy because a person or thing is gone

Soon, Luz started to feel better about being at our school. Luz likes to sing. Luz and I both joined the chorus. Luz has a great voice!

There are many clubs at our school. Luz decided to join the Math Club. She is a math whiz! Since Luz never struggled with math, she is able to help other kids who have trouble with it.

---

chorus: a group of people who sing songs together
whiz: somebody who is very good at something

Luz and I became good friends. We talked and shared our secrets during recess. We visited after school. Sometimes on weekends, our families went out together. I could tell Luz anything. She could keep secrets. She sure was a good friend!

Extend Language   Verb Endings: *-ed, -ing*

*help**ed*** and *help**ing*** are forms of *help*

*miss**ed*** and *miss**ing*** are forms of *miss*

Can you make new words by adding *-ed* and *-ing* to the following verbs? Use a sheet of paper.

Verb	*-ed* form	*-ing* form
look		
talk		
avoid		